GO-BUJ-252

Americans All biographies are inspiring life stories about people of all races, creeds, and nationalities who have uniquely contributed to the American way of life. Highlights from each person's story develop his contributions in his special field — whether they be in the arts, industry, human rights, education, science and medicine, or sports.

Specific abilities, character, and accomplishments are emphasized. Often despite great odds, these famous people have attained success in their fields through the good use of ability, determination, and hard work. These fast-moving stories of real people will show the way to better understanding of the ingredients necessary for personal success.

Jim Thorpe

ALL-AROUND ATHLETE

by George Sullivan

illustrated by Herman B. Vestal

GARRARD PUBLISHING COMPANY
CHAMPAIGN, ILLINOIS

Picture credits:

Culver Pictures: p. 25 (both), 36, 53 (both)
Photoworld: p. 68, 74
United Press International: p. 79, 86
Wide World Photos: p. 2, 89

Copyright © 1971 by George Sullivan

All rights reserved. Manufactured in the U.S.A.

Standard Book Number: 8116-4566-5

Library of Congress Catalog Card Number: 70-135180

Contents

1. The Young Indian

A twig snapped and Jim Thorpe's heart jumped. The boy saw the antlers, then the head—a buck deer.

For more than an hour Jim and his father had been waiting in the thick woods, sitting silent and alert, their rifles beside them. Now their patience had been rewarded.

Jim turned to his father. Mr. Thorpe looked at his son and slowly nodded. Jim knew instantly that he was being put to the test.

His heart beat wildly as he placed the rifle against his shoulder and sighted down the barrel. He knew that if he missed the shot the deer would dart away. Worse yet, he would bitterly disappoint his father.

Jim squeezed the trigger. The rifle's loud report shattered the silence. Jim saw the deer leap crazily, then drop to the ground and lie still.

"I've done it! I've done it!" Jim thought to himself. He wanted to jump up and down and clap his hands, but he did not. Jim was an Indian, a member of the Sauk and Fox tribe, and an Indian would never act like that.

Jim and his father walked to the fallen deer. Neither uttered a word. Mr. Thorpe bent down to examine the kill, then allowed a faint smile to cross his face. He looked up at Jim.

"You will kill many deer, my son," he said.

Jim knew that this was the highest praise. He knew that his father's simple words meant that he had won acceptance as a Sauk and Fox hunter and was a worthy descendant of Chief Black Hawk.

Jim Thorpe, who was to become America's greatest athlete, was born on May 28, 1888, in a two-room farmhouse not far from the Oklahoma settlement of Prague.

His father, Hiram Thorpe, half Sauk and Fox and half Irish, had married a young Indian girl named Charlotte View. She was a great-granddaughter of Chief Black Hawk, the greatest of all Sauk and Fox warriors.

Jim was one of twin boys born to the Thorpes. Charlotte View named one of the babies Wa-Tho-Huck, which means Bright

Path. However, he was christened James Francis Thorpe.

Jim's twin brother was named Charles. They were both husky babies for twins, weighing about five pounds each at birth.

The Thorpe family also included a brother George and two sisters, Mary and Adeline. Later, another boy, Eddie, was born.

The family lived on a 160-acre farm and raised hogs, cattle, and horses. There was always plenty to eat.

Jim's mother often entertained her children with stories about Chief Black Hawk. She told them of his pride and courage and of how he led the Sauk and Fox in their bitter, and sometimes bloody, struggle to retain the lands they owned.

Charlotte View often compared Jim with the legendary Black Hawk. Her son had

Black Hawk's pride and his fighting spirit.

As youngsters, Jim and Charlie were seldom apart. They would climb to the barn roof and jump to the ground. They rode horses and waded in streams.

Of course, they had to attend school. When Jim was six, he and Charlie were enrolled in the Sauk and Fox reservation school. It was located 23 miles from the Thorpe home, so the youngsters had to board there.

Jim did not like leaving the ranch. He missed the hunting and fishing expeditions; he missed Big Hiram. Still, as long as Charlie was with him, it wasn't too bad. They played together by the hour.

The boys always returned to the ranch for summer vacation. There were many chores. The boys worked in the fields and fed the livestock.

Their days were filled with fun, too. Sometimes their father would take Jim and Charlie to the North Canadian River, a few miles from the ranch, for a swim.

Jim's father was a big man. He stood six feet two and weighed 230 pounds. He had remarkable strength. "He could lick any man in our part of the country in wrestling," Jim was to say in later years. He was skilled in every sport. Once the day's chores were done, Big Hiram and the other men in the community would often gather in front of the Thorpe home to wrestle, run, high jump, or broad jump. Jim and Charlie loved to watch them. Big Hiram was almost unbeatable. Jim was very proud of him.

Mr. Thorpe taught his sons how to track game and, with sharp-pointed spears, to fish in the way of their forefathers. He

taught them how to use a rifle. They practiced shooting tree stumps and old tin cans until each boy was a dead shot.

Jim learned to rope and ride a wild pony. There was never a wild one that he couldn't catch, saddle, and ride. The sport made him strong and alert.

One day when Jim was eight, Charlie became ill. His pulse raced and a high fever gripped his small body. The young boy had pneumonia. Day by day his condition became worse. Charlie died.

Charlie's death was a heavy blow to Jim. There was a great emptiness in his life. When it came time for Jim to go off to school alone, he pleaded with Big Hiram to allow him to remain at home. "I can help on the ranch," he said.

Jim knew that Big Hiram had made up his mind. Jim returned to school.

Jim did not make friends easily. Even if he did, who could ever take Charlie's place? The loneliness was more than he could stand. One day, without a word to anyone, Jim walked out of school. He walked and walked, and he did not stop until he reached the Thorpe home.

Big Hiram was standing in the doorway as Jim approached. If he was surprised to see his young son, he did not show it. He waited for Jim to speak.

"I wanted to come home," was all that Jim could think to say.

Big Hiram merely nodded.

"I hope you understand," Jim said weakly.

"You are the one who must understand," said Big Hiram. "You must understand the importance of school."

"Are you going to send me back?" Jim asked.

"I'm not going to *send* you back," Big Hiram said, "I'm going to *take* you back."

He seized Jim's hand and started walking with him in the direction of the school. He walked all 23 miles with Jim. Big Hiram hoped that now the problem was solved.

It was not. Jim left school a second time, but this time Hiram handled the problem in a different way.

"I'm going to send you far away to school," Big Hiram said. "So far that you won't be able to find your way back."

Big Hiram was a man of his word. He sent Jim to Haskell Institute, a school for Indian youngsters operated by the government, in Lawrence, Kansas.

Jim settled into the routine at Haskell without great difficulty. There were no memories of Charlie there to grieve him.

He could not even consider walking away from school, for Haskell was more than 250 miles from home.

In time, Jim became fond of his new school. He had good reasons. At Haskell he saw his first real baseball and football teams. The games fascinated him. Then, too, he became friends with Chauncy Archiquette, Haskell's gridiron hero. Jim idolized him.

Archiquette showed Jim how to hold a football and how to throw it.

"Get your fingers on the laces now," Archiquette instructed Jim. "Hold it tight, really tight." However, Jim's hand was small, and when he threw the ball it traveled no great distance.

Kicking was another matter, however. Archiquette showed Jim how to hold the ball in front of his body, then swing his foot into it. He tossed Jim the ball. "Here, you try it," he said.

Jim boomed the ball down the field. Archiquette watched in awe. "Wow! That's some kick!" he said. Jim felt very proud.

Jim was twelve years old and attending Haskell Institute when his mother was stricken with blood poisoning and died. His mother's death was a big shock to Jim.

He left Haskell Institute to attend a public school only a few miles from the

Thorpe ranch. For a while, he followed a routine of doing schoolwork and ranch chores. Then one day something happened.

An assistant superintendent of the United States Indian Industrial School at Carlisle, Pennsylvania, popularly known as Carlisle Institute, arrived in the North Canadian River Territory of Oklahoma. He was looking for Indian children who might be interested in attending Carlisle. The school had been established in 1879 by the federal government to teach Indian youngsters various trades.

Someone introduced the superintendent to Jim. "What do you want to be when you grow up, young man?" the superintendent asked.

"An electrician," Jim answered.

"Well, we don't have an electrician's school at Carlisle," the superintendent said.

"But we can teach you other trades. How would you like to be a painter, a carpenter, or a tailor?"

Jim smiled half-heartedly. None of these trades really appealed to him. Still, he was a restless young man with an itch to travel, and going to Carlisle would give him a chance to satisfy this urge. He signed up.

Jim was fifteen years old when he reported to Carlisle in the fall of 1904. He was small for his age. He wasn't quite five feet tall, and he weighed only 115 pounds.

Only two months after he arrived at school, Jim received the sad news of Big Hiram's death. He had died of the same illness that had taken Jim's mother. First, Jim had lost his twin brother Charlie. Then his mother had died. Now it was his father.

These were the people he loved most of all. There was no one left.

Despite his grief, Jim shed no tears. The great-great-grandson of Black Hawk would never weep, no matter what happened.

To take his mind off his latest tragedy, Jim turned to sports. He had become an apprentice tailor at Carlisle, and he joined the tailors' football team in the shop league. Jim played guard.

In 1906 the tailors won the league championship. Seven members of the team, including Jim, were then promoted to the varsity squad as scrubs. The scrub team was known as the "Hotshots."

Jim took great pride in being a member of the team. His accomplishments helped him to forget his sadness. For the first time since the death of his father, Jim felt happy.

2. A Fateful Step

Jim returned to Carlisle in the fall eager to continue playing football. One day he was assigned to clean up the practice field where the school's high jumpers were working out.

The bar was set at five feet nine inches —high for those days. The jumpers kept brushing the bar off.

"*I* can jump that high," Jim said.

The athletes looked scornfully at the skinny boy in dungarees. "Let's see you try," said one. "But watch out you don't break your neck."

Jim measured off his distance, then turned and looked at the bar. He sprinted down the short runway and exploded his body over the bar with at least four inches to spare.

Suddenly the track coach was at Thorpe's side. "If you jump like that wearing dungarees and sneakers, you should be able to clear six feet in a track suit and spiked shoes," he said.

"I'd like you to report for track practice tomorrow."

"I can't," Jim said.

The coach's brow wrinkled. "Why not?" he asked.

"I'm playing football with the Hotshots," Jim said. "I'd like to finish the season."

The coach smiled, for he also coached

the Carlisle football team. Maybe I've got a new star here, he thought.

The coach's name was Glenn (Pop) Warner. A big man, with dark, wavy hair, Warner was to become one of the most noted football coaches of all time. He introduced many plays and formations that helped to change the game completely.

"So you play football, too?" Warner said.

Jim nodded.

"Funny, I don't remember seeing you around," Warner said. "But I'll be watching you."

One day not long after, Warner was rebuking his team for its poor tackling. Thorpe, who had been switched from guard to running back, was the man downfield catching punts and returning them against the army of tacklers.

"You've got to get mean," Warner

Young Jim Thorpe, at right, was a gridiron hero for the Carlisle Indian team, below.

shouted. "You've got to hit them hard, so hard they don't get up.

"All right, let's run that drill again," he said. The ball was kicked. Thorpe gathered it in near the goal line, tucked it under his arm, and broke into his graceful hip-swinging stride.

The first man to hit Jim bounced off. A second man did the same. Two others leaped, missed, and wound up clutching handfuls of earth.

Down the field Thorpe raced, swerving and sprinting. He was in the clear! No one was going to stop him now. When Jim crossed into the end zone, his face broke into a wide grin.

Warner beckoned to him. He was not pleased. "What do you think you're doing," the coach barked. "This is supposed to be a tackling practice."

Jim's smile melted in an instant. He met the coach's glare with one of his own. "Nobody tackles Jim," he said slowly.

Warner ordered the drill to be run again. This time the tacklers were able to check Jim's speed, but he still managed to stay on his feet and cross the goal line.

Jim trotted back up the field to where Warner was standing. There was no trace of a smile this time. He flipped the ball to the coach. "Nobody tackles Jim," he repeated. Warner had no answer.

Despite Jim's amazing performance on the practice field, Warner kept him on the sidelines during the early part of the season. This pained Jim. He wanted to be in the thick of the action, hitting the line, throwing his body at the ball carrier, punting, anything. Jim Thorpe wasn't made for sitting on the bench.

Jim finally got his chance. Albert Payne, the team's regular left halfback, injured his knee during an important game against Pennsylvania. Warner put Thorpe in as Payne's replacement.

Under the Warner system, the left halfback was the most important man in the team's attack. In running the ball, he was expected to be able to rip up the middle, pound over the tackles, or sweep around the ends. He was also supposed to punt.

Jim was new to the position and did not know the plays. They gave him the ball and, before he knew what happened, the mammoth Penn line flattened him. Carlisle lost five yards on the play.

"Give it to me again," Jim said in the huddle.

Jim still didn't know the signals. Yet he knew how to run; he knew how to fake a man out of position or stiff-arm him to the ground. Flashing his brilliant speed and elusiveness, Jim carried the ball 65 yards to a touchdown.

Coach Warner counted the Penn tacklers strewn about the playing field. There were seven of them.

The next time the team huddled, Jim was grinning. "That was fun," he announced. "Give it to Jim again."

They kept feeding the ball to Thorpe. Later in the game he streaked 85 yards for another touchdown. Carlisle overwhelmed Penn that day, 26–6.

The Indians went on to whip Harvard and then Minnesota, champions of the Western Conference. Their only loss that season came in a game against Princeton, but it was played on a muddy field, which slowed Thorpe down.

"Jim is just a growing boy," Pop Warner told a newspaper writer. "Sometimes he is lazy and doesn't like to practice. Football is just a good time to Jim, and he gives out his best effort only when he feels like it.

"But you can't keep him on the bench. He has a natural change-of-pace that enables him to float past the defense. His reactions are so fast that sometimes you can't follow them with your eye."

In the spring of 1908 Jim turned his attention to track and field. At the Penn Relays he competed in the high jump and cleared the bar at six feet one, good enough to win first place. He went unbeaten as a sprinter, jumper, and hurdler. He pole-vaulted and threw the hammer.

People were beginning to hear about Jim Thorpe. Carlisle's football team played thirteen games that fall. They won ten, lost two, and tied one. Thorpe was named to Walter Camp's All American third team, earning an important honor for so small a school.

The following spring Thorpe blossomed as a track-and-field star. He seldom could be beaten as a sprinter, hurdler, or jumper. He also starred at lacrosse and was a hard-hitting first baseman for the school baseball team.

Sports were almost Jim's whole life now, and Carlisle was becoming his home.

As spring faded, the students at Carlisle began to make plans for the summer vacation. Jim could not decide what to do.

It was usual for many of the Carlisle students to be assigned to work on farms for the summer. Jim had tried this the summer before, and he did not like it.

One thing was certain: he did not want to go back to Oklahoma. It was not the same without Big Hiram to greet him. It was not home.

Two of Jim's teammates on the Carlisle baseball team, Jesse Young Deer and Joe Libby, came to him with a plan. "We're going down to North Carolina to play baseball this summer," said Jesse. "Why not come along with us?"

Jesse's offer sounded like fun. It was better than going home or doing farm work. "Okay," Jim said. "I'll tag along."

Both Young Deer and Libby were capable outfielders, and they signed on with a team in Rocky Mount. They were paid fifteen dollars a week.

For a time Jim was merely a spectator. Then he began to run out of money. The Rocky Mount manager offered him fifteen dollars a week to play third base. Jim had to eat; he accepted the offer.

It was a decision that was to have a painful effect on Jim's whole life. By accepting money from the Rocky Mount club, Jim became a professional athlete, and thus was no longer eligible for amateur competition.

Jim did not realize this, however. Hundreds of college baseball players of the day signed up to play with little-known professional leagues. Many of the players used false names to deceive officials. Jim did not. "James Francis Thorpe" was the name that appeared on the Rocky Mount roster.

The first game Jim played was at Raleigh, North Carolina. The manager of the Rocky Mount team was wide-eyed as he watched Jim whip the ball across the diamond from his position at third base. The ball traveled with bullet speed and was never off target.

"How'd you like to be a pitcher?" the manager asked Jim one day.

"I'll give it a try," Jim answered.

Jim made a splendid start, hurling a 4–0 shutout. He went on to win 23 games out of the 25 he pitched for Rocky Mount.

Jim went home to Oklahoma after the season was over. He did not go back to Carlisle in the fall. The following spring he signed up with Rocky Mount again.

Major league teams were beginning to hear of Jim's exploits, and the Boston Braves sent a scout to Rocky Mount to watch him pitch. However, by the time the scout arrived, Jim had strained his arm from pitching game after game. The Braves lost interest.

Pop Warner, a great originator of football plays, coached for 44 years.

Jim switched from Rocky Mount to a team in Fayetteville. He had played there only a short while when the league folded because of poor attendance.

Jim returned to Oklahoma. He was not aware that he had broken amateur rules.

Yet the few games of baseball he had played and the small amount of money he had received—never larger than $60 a month—were to cause him great disgrace and grief, and trigger a bitter controversy that has lasted to this day.

Meanwhile, Pop Warner at Carlisle did not know that Jim had been playing baseball. He believed that Thorpe had simply returned to Oklahoma in 1909. In the summer of 1911 Warner wrote to Thorpe.

"If you come back to Carlisle and start training," the letter said, "I think you can make the Olympic team that is going to Stockholm next year."

Jim was overjoyed with the news. He had missed Carlisle, missed his friends and teammates, missed football and the other sports. He counted the days until it was time to leave.

3. College Hero

"Where have you been?" was the first question Pop Warner asked Jim when the young man came back to school.

"Playing ball," Thorpe answered.

Warner didn't bother getting any details. He was too busy marvelling at the change in Jim.

Jim had left Carlisle a boy; he returned a man. He stood six feet one and one-half inches, and he weighed 185 pounds. He had a thick, well-muscled neck, a barrel chest, and thighs like tree trunks. Not only was he bigger, he was faster. Warner smiled to himself. The Olympics were almost a year away. First he would give Big Jim a try with the Carlisle football team.

Jim hadn't touched a football for almost two years, so Warner used him sparingly against Dickinson College in the first game of the season. He played Thorpe only seventeen minutes. In those seventeen minutes Thorpe scored seventeen points, but Jim was just warming up.

The following week against St. Mary's, Thorpe scored three touchdowns. Tough Georgetown was Carlisle's next opponent. Warner didn't use Thorpe until late in the game. Once on the field, Jim followed his usual script, blasting off on a 40-yard touchdown run for the last points in Carlisle's 28–5 win.

The nation's sportswriters were beginning to notice Jim. However, there were still many doubters. "Carlisle has a fine team and one of the best backfield men in the East in Thorpe," wrote one observer, "but the [Carlisle] Braves are stepping out of their class against such powerhouses as Pittsburgh, Pennsylvania, and Harvard."

Jim was told that the newspapers had said that he could be stopped by a first-class team. He listened without showing any emotion, yet inside he was raging.

Pittsburgh was next on Carlisle's schedule. The Panthers were as rough and rugged as any team in the country. Thorpe was determined to show up the newsmen.

He did—but it was no easy task. Pittsburgh was out to "get" Thorpe, and every time Big Jim carried the ball, two, three, or four players piled onto him. He

felt fists, elbows, and knees, yet nothing the Panthers did could erase the good-natured smile from Jim's face.

"This time, left tackle," he would shout to the opposition, and then he'd grab the ball and hurl his body into the spot he had just named.

"Center," he'd call out, and then he'd hit the middle of the line.

Throughout the afternoon he kept challenging the Panthers to stop him, but they couldn't. He leveled the enemy tacklers with his straight-arm or sent them reeling with his quick hip twists.

"Unflustered by ruffianly tactics, Thorpe paced Carlisle to an easy 17–0 victory over Pitt," wrote one of the sportswriters who had underestimated Jim's ability earlier. "The Red Man is all they said he was—and more."

Lafayette was Carlisle's next victim. Jim had another splendid afternoon, scoring two touchdowns and also a field goal in Carlisle's 19–0 victory. Then Penn fell, 16–0, with Jim playing like a demon on defense.

Now the stage was set for the biggest game of the year, Carlisle versus Harvard. There was no better team in football than the Cambridge eleven. The year before they had won eight straight games, scoring 155 points to a mere 5 for the opposition. They were rated the number one team in the country.

Twenty-five thousand fans jammed the Cambridge stadium on the day of the game. Could Thorpe and his teammates topple mighty Harvard? Most people thought not.

Percy Haughton, the Harvard coach, was not impressed by what he had heard and read about Carlisle. He kept his first team on the bench and let second- and third-stringers begin the game.

When the Carlisle team took the field, the crowd noticed that Thorpe's right leg was bandaged. He had injured his ankle in the game against Lafayette, reinjured it against Penn. It was still painfully swollen.

But once the game began, Thorpe seemed not to notice his injury. He booted a thirteen-yard field goal in the first quarter, and a forty-three-yard field goal in the second quarter to give Carlisle six points.

Harvard, meanwhile, answered back with a field goal and a touchdown, and then added an extra point. This gave the Crimson a 9–6 advantage. (A touchdown counted as five points in those days.)

When the third quarter began, Haughton

again kept his first team on the bench. Thorpe was to make him regret his decision.

"Give me the ball," Jim said in the huddle. "I'm going to run with it." No one argued.

Thorpe ripped into the Harvard line, his legs pumping like giant pistons. "Outta my way!" Thorpe yelled, and he charged the Harvard line again and again.

Single-handedly he tore huge holes in the Harvard forward wall. When the defensemen rushed up to meet him, he stiff-armed them into submission. In nine plays, he battered his way 70 yards and into the Harvard end zone. Touchdown!

Jim calmly booted the extra point, sending Carlisle into the lead, 12–9. Later in the quarter Thorpe added to the Carlisle total by kicking another field goal—this one from the 37-yard line. Now Carlisle was on top, 15–9.

The fans were wild with excitement. One cheer blended with the next in an uproar.

Haughton rushed his mammoth regulars into the game, now entering its final stages. Carlisle had the ball on the Harvard 48-yard line.

"Let me boot it," said Thorpe.

"Are you sure, Jim?" asked the Carlisle quarterback. "It's a long way . . . and with your leg."

"Let me boot it," Jim repeated once more.

The crowd grew still as the teams lined up. Thorpe was standing on his own 45-yard line. As the ball was snapped, he took one giant stride, then brought his right toe into the ball. Every pair of eyes followed its flight. It sailed high into the air, then floated in a gentle arc between the uprights. A tremendous roar went up from the stands.

Harvard answered back with a touchdown, but there was no more scoring after that. When the final gun sounded, the scoreboard read: Carlisle 18; Harvard 15.

The game ranks as one of the most stunning upsets in all football history. Jim Thorpe, by scoring every one of his team's eighteen points, was the game's most glorious hero.

The next day the entire student body was on hand at the Carlisle station when the train bearing the team arrived. Jim could hardly believe his eyes. The tumult embarrassed him. He sincerely believed he had not done anything out of the ordinary.

Thorpe's performance that day has seldom been equaled on the American gridiron. Yet Jim Thorpe's day in the sun was just dawning. Even greater days were soon to follow.

4. Olympic Champion

Lulled by the drone of the ship's engines and the warm spring sun, Jim Thorpe dozed peacefully, unmindful of the frantic activity going on about him.

A week before, the steamer *Finland*, carrying America's finest athletes, had left New York bound for Stockholm, Sweden and the Olympic games. In those seven days Jim had seldom left his deck chair.

Runners jogged about the sun deck to keep their legs in shape. Other athletes set up their high-jump bars or laid out broad-jump courses. Big canvas swimming "tanks" were rigged up for the swimmers.

Jim, however, did not take part in the training activity. He *knew* he was ready. Additional running and jumping would achieve nothing, he felt.

"Doesn't he ever train?" one of the athletes asked Pop Warner, who had been named to coach the team.

"Don't worry about him," Warner replied. "He'll be ready when the bell rings."

Legend has it that one day Jim took a piece of chalk and drew a line on the deck. He then walked off 23 feet, a distance he judged would be sufficient to win the running broad-jump competition, and at that point he drew a second line.

"Hey, fellows," one of Jim's teammates called out. "Look at this. Big Jim is about to go to work."

Not at all. Thorpe surveyed the distance carefully. Then he turned abruptly and went back to his deck chair.

When Thorpe arrived in Stockholm and the actual competition began, the stocky Indian quickly showed that his shipboard holiday had not impaired his skills.

No athlete has ever faced a more difficult challenge than Jim Thorpe did in the 1912 Olympic Games. During the tryouts, an Olympic official asked Jim, "How many events do you want to enter?"

"All of them," Jim answered. "It's no fun watching."

Jim managed to compete in "all of them" by entering both the pentathlon and decathlon. The pentathlon consisted of five different track-and-field events. The decathlon was twice as demanding, consisting of ten different track-and-field events.

Since 1924 only the decathlon has been offered Olympic trackmen. Thus Thorpe, by competing in a total of fifteen events, faced a test that is without equal in modern times.

Jim opened his quest for the pentathlon championship by winning the broad jump with a leap of 23 feet, 2-7/10 inches. He then won the 200-meter sprint, covering the distance in 22.9 seconds. The javelin throw came next; Jim finished third. He then won the 1,500-meter run with a time of 4 minutes, 44.8 seconds, and captured the discus competition with a throw of 116 feet, 8-4/10 inches.

With this brilliant showing, Jim easily won the pentathlon title. His point total was twice as high as his nearest rival's.

So far Jim had been merely remarkable. In the decathlon contest he was incredible.

Well ahead of the other contestants, Jim crosses the 200-meter race finish line. Below he is shown throwing the javelin.

He won four decathlon events—the high hurdles in 15.6 seconds; the 1,500-meter run in 4 minutes, 40.1 seconds; the high jump with a leap of 6 feet, 1-6/10 inches; and the shot put with a toss of 42 feet, 5-9/20 inches. He was third in the 100-meter dash, the discus throw, the pole vault, and the broad jump. He was placed fourth in the 400-meter races and the javelin throw.

Jim scored a total of 8,412.96 points. Hugo Wieslander of Sweden, the second place man, finished almost 700 points behind Jim.

Thorpe's dazzling feat in winning both the pentathlon and decathlon had never before been achieved in the history of sport.

At a victory stand in the center of the magnificent gray brick and granite stadium, King Gustav V of Sweden summoned the winners forward, one by one.

"To James Thorpe . . ." the king said, ". . . for winning the pentathlon."

Jim stepped forward proudly, his head high. Smiling warmly, the king presented the young man with a bronze bust in the monarch's likeness and a gold medal. The crowd broke into thunderous applause.

"To James Thorpe . ." the king said a second time, ". . . for winning the decathlon."

Jim stood arrow-straight, scarcely breathing. This time the king handed him a magnificent gold and jewel-encrusted chalice, cast in the shape of a Viking ship, a prize awarded by the czar of Russia. Again he received a gold medal for first place. Loud cheers shook the vast stadium.

Then the king took a large laurel wreath and carefully draped it over Jim's shoulders. As he did, the king uttered these words: "You, sir, are the greatest athlete in the world."

You, sir, are the greatest athlete in the world. There could be no higher praise.

Yet these words of tribute were only the beginning for Jim Thorpe. He returned to the United States an all-conquering hero.

Mammoth throngs roared a welcome to him in New York City. President William Howard Taft called him "the highest type of citizen." Newspaper headlines shrieked his name. The students at Carlisle Institute went wild when he arrived.

You, sir, are the greatest athlete in the world.

King Gustav's statement was not an exaggeration. The world of sport has never seen the equal of this proud Sauk and Fox Indian from the plains of Oklahoma.

56

5. "Guilty!"

Once back at Carlisle, Jim plunged into the fall sports program. It was time for football. Again Jim showed himself to be a superman of the gridiron.

In a game against Dickinson College, only Thorpe's long punts kept Dickinson from scoring. Once more Thorpe dropped back to kick, this time standing in the Carlisle end zone. Then disaster; the pass from center was bad, sailing over Jim's head. Jim scampered after the loose ball as Dickinson tacklers poured in.

Finally Jim managed to scoop up the ball. He shook one tackler and then another. He broke out of the end zone and streaked for the Dickinson end of the field. He sidestepped or straight-armed every man who came for him, and he did not stop running until he had crossed the Dickinson goal line. He had traveled 110 yards! Carlisle went on to chalk up an easy win.

Against Lehigh it was more of the same. Jim intercepted a pass and took the ball the length of the field for a touchdown, a 105-yard run. Again Carlisle won with ease.

The Indians went on to trounce Syracuse and Pittsburgh. Late in the season, Carlisle faced Army, one of the toughest teams in the East.

Thorpe had been scoring touchdowns at a record rate. The cadets knew that in order to defeat Carlisle they would have to stop Jim. "Get that Indian!" became the Army battle cry.

Still, Jim could not be stopped. In the first quarter he scored a touchdown on a running play, and when he crossed the goal line he carried three West Point tacklers with him.

One Army player painfully twisted his knee trying to tackle Thorpe. He had to be helped from the field, and he never played football again. The player's name was Dwight D. Eisenhower.

"Thorpe gained ground; he *always* gained ground," Eisenhower was to say years later in recalling the game. "He was the greatest man I ever saw."

Perhaps Eisenhower had in mind a play that occurred late in the game. Thorpe took an Army punt on the Carlisle 10-yard

line and went the 90 yards for a touchdown.

The Indians, however, had been off side
on the play. The touchdown was nullified,
and Army got a chance to kick again.

This time Thorpe caught the ball on the
Carlisle 5-yard line. Again he scored, this
time with a run of 95 yards.

"That has to be the longest run I ever
made," Jim said to a teammate. "I went
185 yards for just one touchdown."

Thorpe scored 22 points against Army
that day. Carlisle won, 27–6.

For the 1912 season, Jim scored a total
of 25 touchdowns and 168 points. No
player since has approached these records.

One day toward the end of the football
season, a frowning Pop Warner called Jim
into his office. He motioned Jim to take a
seat.

"Did you play baseball in Rocky Mount and Fayetteville?" the coach asked.

"Sure I did," Jim said. "I told you that."

"But did you get paid for it?" said Warner.

"Sure," Jim said. "Everyone did."

Warner's face turned grim. "Don't you know that you're an amateur, Jim, and amateurs aren't supposed to get paid?"

Jim scratched his head. "But everybody plays baseball and gets paid for it," Jim said. "What's so wrong about that?"

Then Warner explained that the Amateur Athletic Union (the A.A.U.), the governing body of amateur sports in the United States, had learned that Jim had received money for playing baseball.

"It's quite a serious matter," said the coach. "If they judge that you have broken amateur rules, you will be disciplined."

Soon A.A.U. officials were to meet to consider Jim's case. Jim wrote to the A.A.U. to explain his side of the dispute.

"I did not play for the money that was in it, but because I like to play ball," Jim's letter said. "I was not very wise to the ways of the world and did not realize that I was doing wrong.

"I hope I will be partly excused by the fact that I was simply an Indian school boy and did not know that I was doing wrong, because I was doing what many other college men had done, except that they did not use their own names."

Soon after, the A.A.U. announced that it had reached a decision. Its verdict: "Guilty."

Jim's sentence was harsh. He was to be stripped of the title "champion." His name was to be removed from the Olympic record book. He was ordered to return all the medals and trophies he had received, including the bronze bust of King Gustav and the great gold trophy in the shape of a Viking ship.

The average American resented the A.A.U.'s action, feeling it cruelly unfair. "He's the greatest athlete in the world," was a typical reaction. "How can it take his medals away from him?"

At Jim's request, Pop Warner crated up the sculptured head of the king of Sweden and the Viking ship and sent them back to Sweden. Today they are to be found on display in the Olympic Museum in Lausanne, Switzerland.

Ferdinand R. Bie of Norway, the man who finished second in the pentathlon, was declared the winner. When officials went to present him with the championship medal, Bie said: "Thorpe won the pentathlon. The medal belongs to him."

Hugo Wieslander of Sweden, who was named the decathlon champion in place of Thorpe, was awarded the medal for this competition. "I didn't win the decathlon," Wieslander said. "Thorpe did. The medal belongs to him."

Jim did not protest the A.A.U.'s decision. The Sauk and Fox are a proud people. They had been made to suffer and die and accept the loss of their lands. They did not whine. Jim was a true Sauk and Fox, and his pride would not allow him to speak out.

Besides, he had a new world to conquer. Professional sports were beckoning him. Here was a new challenge, a new opportunity.

6. The Wonderful Years

One afternoon not long after Jim's final appearance in a Carlisle football uniform, the telephone rang in Pop Warner's office. John McGraw, the fiery manager of baseball's New York Giants, was on the line.

"I hear you've got a pretty good prospect down there," McGraw said.

"If you're talking about Thorpe, he's the world's best," Warner replied. "But if you want him, you'd better make a good offer right away, or you're going to have to be bidding against just about every other team in major league baseball."

Indeed, it was true. No less than four other big league teams wanted Jim to sign —the Chicago White Sox, the St. Louis Browns, the Cincinnati Reds, and the Pittsburgh Pirates. Two of these clubs had sent scouts to Carlisle to try to get Jim's name on a contract.

McGraw had hoped he was going to be able to sign Thorpe at a bargain price. He

Manager John McGraw stands by as Thorpe signs a three-year contract to play with the New York Giants.

didn't like "college boys" in the first place, and the fact that this one was going to cost him a great deal of money made matters worse.

"Let me talk to the Indian himself," McGraw snapped.

Jim took the phone. "I hear from our scouts that you're a pretty good ballplayer," he heard McGraw say.

Jim did not answer. He knew he was better than "pretty good," but he was not one to proclaim his own talents.

"I'd like you to join our team," McGraw went on. "It's a tough, running, fighting team, and we can use a player like you. We'll pay you $4,500 a year on a three-year contract."

A salary of $4,500 a year was excellent for the time. Only the very best players earned that much. However, the figure did not impress Jim. "That's what some of the other teams have offered me," he said.

McGraw, realizing that Jim would be an outstanding gate attraction, had no choice but to raise the offer. "We'll add another $500 for expenses," said McGraw. "That's $5,000 a year. What do you say?"

"Okay," said Jim. "I'll take it."

The next spring Jim reported for training at the Giants' camp at Marlin Springs, Texas. The New Yorkers had won the National League championship in both 1911 and 1912, and their lineup was brimming with stars.

Jim hit well and fielded well during the exhibition season, but he could not win a starting role. McGraw believed in hard work and diligent practice. Jim did not. Baseball was fun. He played the game because he enjoyed it. "Why make hard work

out of having fun?" he thought. As a result, Jim and his manager often crossed swords.

One day Jim was roughhousing with big Jim Tesreau, one of the New York pitchers. "I'll bet you can't throw me down," said Tesreau.

Jim grinned and bent into a wrestler's crouch. The two grappled for several minutes. Finally Jim pinned Tesreau to the clubhouse floor. Tesreau came out of the contest with a sprained shoulder and could not pitch. McGraw was furious when he got the news. "That Indian," he muttered over and over through clenched teeth.

Once the season began, McGraw did not use Thorpe very often. The idleness caused Jim to develop an even greater disregard for training rules. The feud between Jim and McGraw grew hotter. The two men often exchanged bitter words.

Before the season was very old, McGraw sent Thorpe to the minor leagues, to a team in Milwaukee. Jim played there for most of the 1913 and 1914 seasons. In 1915 McGraw assigned Jim to a New York farm club in Harrisburg, Pennsylvania.

During his first season at Milwaukee, Jim had married Iva Miller, who had attended Carlisle with him. Three daughters,

Gale, Charlotte, and Frances, and a son, James, Jr., were born.

Jim adored the boy. Then in 1917 little Jim was struck with infantile paralysis. The disease took his life.

Thorpe went on a wild rampage. He disappeared and no one could find him.

Then suddenly he was back and playing baseball. Outwardly he seemed not to have changed. He wore the familiar wide grin and joked with his teammates. Still, there was a fresh scar inside.

The relationship between the prideful Thorpe and the hot-tempered McGraw was never peaceful. Matters between the two reached a climax in 1919. Jim had started the season in right field for the Giants and had been hitting like a demon. Nevertheless McGraw benched him. "I'm going to give Red Murray a try," the manager said.

Jim practices his swing before going up
to bat for the Giants.

Jim bristled with anger. He said nothing.

Late in the game, the Giants needed a run desperately. McGraw looked over to where Thorpe was sitting. "Go up and hit for Murray," ordered the manager.

"Why not let Murray hit?" Thorpe said sarcastically as he picked up his bat. "He can do better than Big Jim."

McGraw's anger smoldered. What happened next made him explode.

The first ball came in. Jim swung at it almost without looking, missing the pitch by a mile. He did the very same thing on the next two pitches. Then Jim strode back to the bench.

He glared at McGraw. "I told you Murray was a better man," he declared.

McGraw blew up. Shortly after, he traded Jim to Boston.

In Boston the playful Thorpe found a kindred spirit in the zany Walter (Rabbit) Maranville, the team's shortstop. Thorpe and the Rabbit dropped water-filled paper bags out of hotel windows onto the heads of pedestrians. One night they climbed a tree and imitated howling bobcats until the police came and silenced them.

Once Maranville and Thorpe returned to their hotel about dawn after a night on the town. Maranville spotted a gurgling fountain in the hotel lobby that contained several goldfish. "Oh, boy, food!" Maranville cried out, and he leaped into the water. Before anyone could stop him, he devoured a fish raw.

Thorpe and Maranville together were more than any one manager could handle. The next year Thorpe was shipped down to the minor leagues again, this time to

Akron. The following season it was Toledo, Ohio, then Portland, Oregon, and the next season Hartford, Connecticut.

Often it was said that Thorpe's career in baseball was hampered because he could not hit a curve ball. Thorpe himself always scoffed at this criticism. "My last season in the major leagues I hit .327," he once pointed out, "so I must have hit a couple of curve balls."

For several years beginning in 1915, Jim played both baseball and football. After the baseball season ended in 1915, Jim took a job as an assistant football coach at the University of Indiana. While there he received an offer from the Canton (Ohio) Bulldogs to play professional football.

The pro game was then a great deal different than it is today. Interest in the sport was centered in the mining towns of Pennsylvania and the industrial cities of Ohio and New York. There was no league, no organization. Often players were paid out of what could be collected at the games by passing the hat among the fans.

Jack Cusack, who owned the Canton team, offered Thorpe $500 a game to play and to help coach. Thorpe didn't stop to think whether the offer was a good one or not. He longed to get his hands on the ball again, to hit the line, to sweep an end.

"You're paying Thorpe too much," Cusack was advised. "You're going to bankrupt the club."

Cusack believed, however, there was magic in Jim Thorpe's name, and that big crowds would pay to see him play. Cusack was right. Canton had been averaging around 1,200 fans per game before signing Thorpe. The first time Jim appeared in the Canton lineup, the attendance climbed to 6,000. It went to 8,000 for the next game.

Late in the season the Bulldogs turned back their traditional rivals, the Massillon (Ohio) Tigers, 6–0, on a pair of field goals by Thorpe. The victory gave Canton the world's professional football championship.

Star halfback of the Canton Bulldogs, Jim lunges forward to tackle his opponent.

In 1920 the owners of the best-known professional teams of the day met to form an organized league, which was to become the National Football League. They elected Thorpe the league's first president. The role of an executive did not appeal to Thorpe, however. He quit as president the next year to devote his full time to playing.

Thorpe was now thirty-two, but he demonstrated that time had not damaged his skills to any great degree. As for his pride, it had not diminished in the slightest.

One day Jim led the Bulldogs into Chicago for a game against the Bears. The game was played on a field where the end zones sloped sharply down and away from the goalposts.

During the game Chicago had to punt from its own end zone. George Halas, coach of the Chicago team, asked Thorpe if it would be all right if the Chicago punter came out of the end zone to kick. "We'll give you back the yardage after the kick return," Halas explained.

"Sure," said Thorpe. "Go ahead."

Later in the game Thorpe's team fumbled the ball right in front of their own goalposts. Now they would have to punt from *their* end zone.

Thorpe walked over to where Halas was standing. "Is it okay if I come out of the end zone to punt?" he asked.

Halas' team had never beaten the Bulldogs. "Here's our big chance," he thought. He looked at Thorpe stonily.

"Are you kidding?" Halas said. "The answer is no!"

Thorpe didn't say a word, but inside he was raging.

"I'm going to kick anyway," Thorpe announced to his teammates in the huddle.

Thorpe stood on the sloping ground, his arms outstretched, waiting for the ball. His face was now a grim mask. When the ball came, Thorpe took one long stride and then, with all the power he could muster, he swung his right foot into the ball. It

boomed into the sky, spiraling over the heads of the players. No one was near when the ball came back to earth far downfield. After it struck, it kept rolling and rolling. Finally it stopped—on the Bears' three-yard line. Jim's punt had traveled more than one hundred yards, an incredible feat.

Many stories are told about Jim's career in professional football. One of the most famous of them concerns Knute Rockne.

Rockne, in the days before he became a famous coach at the University of Notre Dame, played end for the Massillon Tigers. One day the Tigers faced the Canton Bulldogs before a sellout crowd. Rockne made up his mind to cool off Thorpe. On the first play from scrimmage, Rockne ripped through the Bulldog line to topple Thorpe with a pile-driving tackle.

As he got to his feet, Thorpe looked at Rockne with displeasure. "You shouldn't do that to Jim," Thorpe said. Then he pointed to the stands. "All those people came here to see Jim run."

Rockne snickered. "Well, go ahead and run—if you can," he answered.

Thorpe took the ball again, and Rockne

promptly smashed him to the ground a second time. "I told you, Rock," said Thorpe, "these people came to see Big Jim run."

Thorpe called for the ball a third time. Rockne came blazing in. Thorpe artfully eluded the charge, then unleashed a hip and a stiff-arm. Rockne went down, never knowing what hit him, while Thorpe breezed 60 yards for a touchdown.

As he trotted back to the Canton bench to the cheers of the crowd, Thorpe saw the dazed and bleeding Rockne being helped from the field. Thorpe went over to him. "That's a good boy, Rock," he said. "You sure let Jim run."

Season after season the fans poured out to see Thorpe. He earned as much as $15,000 a year with such clubs as the Bulldogs, the Cleveland Indians, the Oorang

Big Jim's powerful punt sends a football
sailing across the field.

Indians (of La Rue, Ohio), the Toledo Maroons, and the Rock Island (Illinois) Independents.

Thorpe, in his later years, held fond memories of his days as a professional football star. Many of his teammates from Carlisle had joined him on the Bulldogs —players like Pete Calac, Joe Guyon, Little Twig, Red Fox, and Long Time Sleep.

"We didn't lose a ball game for three or four seasons," Thorpe once recalled. "Those were the wonderful years."

7. Unconquerable Indian

The 1920s have been called the Golden Age of Sport. They were not golden years for Jim Thorpe, however.

Thorpe was aging. His skills were no longer a match for his fighting spirit. Yet he continued to play the game he loved.

He sunk deep into baseball's minor leagues, playing in almost complete obscurity. He continued playing football, too. In 1929, at the age of 41, he played for pro football's Chicago Cardinals in the annual Thanksgiving Day game against the Bears, but he showed only brief glimpses of his once mighty talents.

October 1929 brought the Great Depression, a period of feeble business activity which lasted through most of the 1930s. Millions of people could not find work.

It was a sad period for Jim. He settled down in California. He got part-time jobs playing minor roles in motion pictures.

He toured the country giving lectures

Phil (left) and Bill Thorpe (right) learn football skills from their famous father.

on football. People flocked to hear him, and they listened with respect.

A moment of glory came in 1932. That year the Olympic Games were held in Los Angeles. Jim sat in the presidential box, a guest of Vice-President Charles Curtis. When Jim was introduced, the crowd of more than 100,000 people who filled the mammoth stadium rose as one to give him a thunderous ovation. It was an unforgettable moment.

Some difficult days followed but Jim never complained. He faced the bad times with courage.

During World War II, Jim tried to enlist in the armed services, but he was turned down. "You're too old," he was told. So he joined the merchant marine and was given duty as a crew member aboard an ammunition ship bound for India.

From time to time through the years, efforts were made to have Jim's medals and trophies returned to him and to have his name restored as the 1912 Olympic penthathlon and decathlon champion. All such efforts were in vain.

The matter never caused Jim to be bitter. He took a secret pride in what he had achieved. He knew that no one would ever forget his victories, even though the records had been removed from the book. Thorpe was right.

In 1963, Thorpe was one of the first men named to the Pro Football Hall of Fame in Canton, Ohio. In 1969, when the National Football League celebrated its first fifty years, Thorpe was chosen as a member of the All Pro All Star Team for the 1920s. The same year he was similarly honored by college football.

In 1950, a few years before Thorpe's death, the Associated Press took a poll to determine "the greatest of all sports figures of the first half of the twentieth century." Ballots were sent out to sportswriters and broadcasters in every part of the country.

Two out of every three ballots came back with an "X" beside the name Jim Thorpe. Jim received 252 first-place votes. The great Babe Ruth received only 86 first-place votes.

Jim died of a heart attack at his trailer home in Lomita, California, in 1953. He was sixty-five.

He died, however, secure in the knowledge that his exploits would never be forgotten, that in the hearts and minds of Americans he was, as King Gustav had said, "the greatest athlete in the world."

Index

94

with Rocky Mount, 33-36
with Toledo Maroons, 87
Thorpe, Mary (sister), 10
Toledo Maroons, 87

United States Indian School.
See Carlisle Institute
United States Military
Academy, 59-61

Warner, Glenn (Pop), 24,
26, 27, 28, 29, 31, 37
(pic), 38, 39, 50, 61,
62, 65, 67
Western Conference, 29
Wieslander, Hugo, 54, 66

Young Deer, Jesse, 33